MW01093344

Opera Journeys Libretto Series

Giuseppe Verdi's

*R*IGOLETTO

COMPLETE LIBRETTO
with Music Highlight examples

Edited by Burton D. Fisher
Principal lecturer, *Opera Journeys Lecture Series*

Opera Journeys Publishing™/Boca Raton, Florida

Copyright © 2002, 2013 by Opera Journeys Publishing

All rights reserved

No part of this publication may be reproduced, stored in a retrieval system, or transmitted, in any form or by any means, electronic, mechanical, photocopying, recording, or otherwise, without the prior permission of the authors.

All musical notations contained herein are original transcriptions by Opera Journeys Publishing.

Printed in the United States of America

WEB SITE: www.operajourneys.com   **E MAIL: operaj@bellsouth.net**

Rigoletto

Opera in Italian in three acts

Music
by
Giuseppe Verdi

Libretto by Francesco Maria Piave,
based on Victor Hugo's play
Le Roi s'amuse,
("The King Has a Good Time")

Premiere at the Gran Teatro La Fenice, Venice,
March 1851

RIGOLETTO

Libretto

Act I - Scene 1

A magnificent and sumptuous hall in the palace of the Duke of Mantua.
Ladies, gentlemen, and pages pass through the hall. Others dance in the inner rooms.
The Duke and the courtier Borsa are deep in conversation.

Allegro con brio

Duke:
Della mia bella incognita borghese
toccare il fin dell'avventura io voglio.

Duke:
I'll soon succeed in my adventure with
that unknown woman.

Borsa:
Di quella giovin che vedete al tempio?

Borsa:
Is it that young woman you saw in
church?

Duca:
Da tre mesi ogni festa.

Duke:
I've been following her every Sunday for
three months.

Borsa:
La sua dimora?

Borsa:
Where does she live?

Duca:
In un remoto calle; misterioso un uom
v'entra ogni notte.

Duke:
In an obscure street; a strange man enters
the house every night.

Borsa:
E sa colei chi sia l'amante suo?

Borsa:
Does she know that you want to be her
lover?

Duca:
Lo ignora.

Duke:
She's unaware of my intentions.

A group of ladies and gentlemen pass before the Duke and Borsa.

Borsa:
Quante beltà! Mirate.

Borsa:
What beauty! Look at them.

Duca:
Le vince tutte di Cepran la sposa.

Duke:
Ceprano's wife is the most beautiful.

Borsa:
Non v'oda il conte, o Duca.

Borsa: *(aside to the Duke)*
Duke, don't let her husband hear you.

Duca:
A me che importa?

Duke:
Why should I care?

Borsa:
Dirlo ad altra ei potria.

Borsa:
He might tell another woman.

Duca:
Né sventura per me certo saria.

Duke:
It wouldn't be a misfortune for me.

Allegretto
DUKE

Questa o quella   per me pari so- no a quant'altre d'intor - no,

Questa o quella per me pari sono a
quant'altre d'intorno, d'intorno mi vedo;
del mio core l'impero non cedo meglio ad
una che ad altra beltà.

This woman or that woman, they're all
the same. I'm surrounded by so many.
My heart never ceases to want to conquer
one beauty or another.

La costoro avvenenza è qual dono di che
il fato ne infiora la vita; s'oggi questa mi
torna gradita, forse un'altra, forse un'altra
doman lo sarà, un'altra, forse un'altra
doman lo sarà.

Love is a gift, a fate that embellishes and
invigorates life; if today this one is
disagreeable, perhaps another, perhaps it
will be another tomorrow, perhaps there
will be another tomorrow.

La costanza, tiranna del core, detestiamo
qual morbo, qual morbo crudele;
sol chi vuole si serbe fidele; non v'ha
amor, se non v'è libertà.

Fidelity is a cruel disease, a tyranny of
the heart, and a disease we detest;
if one wants to be faithful, there is no
love, and there is no freedom.

De' mariti il geloso furore, degli amanti le
smanie derido; anco d'Argo i cent'occhi
disfido se mi punge, se mi punge una
qualche beltà, se mi punge una qualche
beltà.

I mock marital jealousies with a fury;
I challenge the hundred eyes of Argus
because if a woman stings me, she stings
me with some of her beauty.

Ladies and gentlemen dance a Minuet.
The Countess Ceprano passes before the Duke, and he addresses her gallantly.

Duca:
Partite? Crudele!

Duke: *(to the Countess)*
Are you leaving? How cruel of you!

Contesa de Ceprano:
Seguire lo sposo m'è forza a Ceprano.

Countess Ceprano:
It is my duty to follow my husband.

Duca:
Ma dee luminoso in Corte tal astro qual
sole brillare. Per voi qui ciascuno dovrà
palpitare. Per voi già possente la fiamma
d'amore, inebria, conquide, distrugge il
mio core.

Duke:
You are the most radiant of all the
beauties of the Court. My heart throbs to
possess you. The flame of love has
intoxicated me and conquered my heart.

The Duke fervently kisses the Countess's hand.

Contessa di Ceprano:
Calmatevi.

Countess Ceprano:
Calm yourself.

Duca:
La fiamma d'amore inebria, conquide,
distrugge il mio core.

Duke:
The flame of love has intoxicated me and
conquered my heart.

Contessa di Ceprano:
Calmatevi, calmatevi.

Countess Ceprano:
Calm yourself. Calm yourself.

Duca:
Per voi già possente la fiamma d'amore
inebria, conquide, distrugge il mio core.

Duke:
To possess you, the flame of love has
intoxicated me and conquered my heart.

The Duke offers his arm to the Countess. As both leave, Rigoletto enters.

Rigoletto:
In testa che avete, signor di Ceprano?

Rigoletto: *(sarcastically to Ceprano)*
What disturbs you, lord Ceprano?

Ceprano gestures that he is agitated. He follows the Duke and the Countess.

Rigoletto:
Ei sbuffa! Vedete?

Rigoletto: *(to the courtiers)*
He's fuming! Did you see him?

Cortigiani:
Che festa!

Courtiers:
What amusement!

Rigoletto:
Oh sì!

Rigoletto:
Oh indeed!

Borsa:
Il Duca qui pur si diverte!

Borsa:
The Duke indeed finds pleasures here!

Rigoletto:
Così non è sempre?
Che nuove scoperte!
Il giuoco ed il vino, le feste, la danza,
battaglie, conviti, ben tutto gli sta.

Or della Contessa l'assedio egli avanza, e
intanto il marito fremendo ne va.

Rigoletto:
And when isn't it that way?
What new adventures he discovers!
Wherever he goes, there's always games,
wine, amusement, the dance,
battles, banquets.
Now he advances and seizes the
Countess, and the cuckolded husband is
trembling from his misfortune.

Cynically laughing, Rigoletto departs. Marullo enters eagerly.

Marullo:
Gran nuova! Gran nuova!

Marullo:
I've great news! Great news!

Borsa:
Che avvenne? Parlate!

Borsa:
What happened? Tell us?

Marullo:
Stupir ne dovrete.

Marullo:
You'll be astonished.

Borsa:
Narrate, narrate!

Borsa:
Tell us, tell us!

Marullo:
Ah, ah! Rigoletto.

Marullo: *(laughing)*
Ha, ha! It's about Rigoletto.

Borsa:
Ebben?

Borsa:
Well?

Marullo:
Caso enorme!

Marullo:
It's incredible!

Borsa:
Perduto ha la gobba?
Non è più difforme?

Borsa:
Has he lost his hunchback?
He's no longer deformed?

Marullo:
Più strana è la cosa!
Il pazzo possiede....

Marullo: *(very seriously)*
The truth is even stranger!
The crazy fool has....

Borsa:
Infine?

Borsa:
Treasures?

Marullo:
Un'amante!

Marullo:
He has a lover!

Borsa:
Un'amante! Chi il crede?

Borsa: *(surprised)*
A lover! Who would believe that?

Marullo:
Il gobbo in Cupido or s'è trasformato.

Marullo:
The hunchback has become Cupid.

Borsa:
Quel mostro? Cupido!

Borsa:
Isn't he a monster? Cupid!

Borsa, Marullo:
Cupido beato!

Borsa, Marullo:
A blessed Cupid!

The Duke returns, followed by Rigoletto, and then Ceprano.
The Duke addresses Rigoletto.

Duca:
Ah, più di Ceprano importuno non v'è.
La cara sua sposa è un angiol per me!

Duke:
Ceprano's presence here annoys me.
His dear wife is an angel for me!

Rigoletto:
Rapitela.

Rigoletto:
Abduct her.

Duca:
È detto; ma il farlo?

Duke:
That's easy to say; but how can I do it?

Rigoletto:
Sta sera.

Rigoletto:
Do it tonight.

Duca:
Non pensi tu al conte?

Duke:
What about her husband?

Rigoletto:
Non c'è la prigione?

Rigoletto:
What about prison?

Duca:
Ah no.

Duke:
Oh, no.

Rigoletto:
Ebben, s'esilia.

Rigoletto:
Well, exile him.

Duca:
Nemmeno, buffone.

Duke:
Never, that's ridiculous.

Rigoletto:
Allora, allora la testa.

Conte di Ceprano:
(Oh l'anima nera!)

Duca:
Che dì, questa testa?

Rigoletto:
È ben naturale! Che far di tal testa?
A cosa ella vale?

Conte di Ceprano:
Marrano!

Duca:
Fermate!

Rigoletto:
Da rider mi fa.

Marullo:
In furia è montato!

Duca:
Buffone, vien qua.

Borsa:
In furia è montato!

Marullo:
In furia è montato!

Cortigiani:
In furia è montato!

Duca:
Ah sempre tu spingi lo scherzo
all'estremo.

Conte di Ceprano:
Vendetta del pazzo!Contr'esso un rancore
di noi chi non ha?

Rigoletto: *(gesturing decapitation)*
Then, then his head.

Count Ceprano: *(aside)*
(What an evil soul!)

Duke: *(tapping the Count's shoulder)*
Will your head yield easily?

Rigoletto:
Naturally! What to do with that head?
Will she appreciate it?

Count Ceprano: *(grasping his sword)*
You devil!

Duke: *(to Ceprano)*
Stop!

Rigoletto: *(to Ceprano)*
You're making me laugh.

Marullo: *(discussing Ceprano)*
His anger is mounting!

Duke: *(to Rigoletto)*
Jester, come here.

Borsa:
His anger is mounting!

Marullo:
His anger is mounting!

Courtiers:
His anger is mounting!

Duke: *(to Rigoletto)*
You always push your joking to extremes.

Count Ceprano: *(to the courtiers)*
A merciless revenge! Who among you
hasn't been the victim of his vindictiveness?

Rigoletto:
Che coglier mi puote?
Di loro non temo.

Rigoletto:
What is this gathering planning for me?
I don't fear them.

Duca:
Quell'ira che sfidi, colpir ti potrà.

Duke:
The anger you have aroused will strike
back at you.

Conte di Ceprano:
Vendetta! In armi chi ha core.

Count Ceprano:
Vengeance! And with arms if you have
the courage.

Borsa, Marullo:
Ma come?

Borsa, Marullo:
But how?

Rigoletto:
Del duca il protetto nessun toccherà.

Rigoletto:
I am protected by the Duke, and no one
can touch me.

Conte di Ceprano:
Doman sia da me. A notte.

Count Ceprano:
Tomorrow join me. At night.

Borsa, Marullo:
Sì. Sarà.

Borsa, Marullo:
Yes. We'll be there.

Duca:
Ah sempre tu spingi....

Duke:
You always push too much....

Rigoletto:
Che coglier mi puote?
Di loro non temo.

Rigoletto:
What is this gathering planning for me?
I don't fear them.

Borsa, Marulla, Conte di Ceprano:
Vendetta del pazzo! Contr'esso un
rancore

Borsa, Marullo, Count Ceprano:
A merciless revenge! Who among you
hasn't been the victim of his vindictiveness?

Duca:
Lo scherzo all'estremo....

Duke:
The excessive joking....

Rigoletto:
Del duca il protetto nessun toccherà, no,
no....

Rigoletto:
I am protected by the Duke, and no one
can touch me, no, no.....

Borsa, Marullo, Conte di Ceprano:
Pei tristi suoi modi di noi chi non ha?

Borsa, Marullo, Count Ceprano:
Who among you hasn't been the victim
of his vindictiveness?

Duca:
Ah sempre tu spingi lo scherzo
all'estremo....

Duke:
You always push your joking to
extremes....

Rigoletto:
Nessun, nessuno, nessun, nessuno.

Rigoletto:
No, one, no one, no one, no one.

Conte di Ceprano:
Vendetta! Vendetta!

Count Ceprano:
Vengeance! Vengeance!

Borsa, Marullo:
Vendetta! Vendetta!

Borsa:
Vengeance! Vengeance!

Duca:
Quell'ira che sfidi, quell'ira che sfidi,
colpir ti potrà.

Duke:
The anger you have aroused will strike
back at you.

Rigoletto:
nessun, nessuno del duca il protetto,
nessuno toccherà.

Rigoletto:
No one, no one, I am protected by the
Duke, and no one can touch me.

Conte di Ceprano:
Vendetta! Sta notte chi ha core sia in armi
da me.

Count Ceprano:
Vengeance! Tonight those who have
courage bear arms with me.

Borsa, Marullo:
Vendetta! Sì! A notte sarà.

Borsa, Marullo:
Vengeance! Yes, It will be tonight!

Duca:
Ah sempre tu spingi....

Duke:
You always push too much....

Rigoletto:
Che coglier mi puote?
Di loro non temo....

Rigoletto:
What is this gathering planning for me?
I don't fear them....

Borsa, Marullo, Conte di Ceprano:
Vendetta del pazzo! Contr'esso un
rancore....

Borsa, Marullo, Count Ceprano:
A merciless revenge! Who among you
hasn't been the victim....

Duca:
Lo scherzo all'estremo....

Duke:
The joking is excessive....

Rigoletto:
Del duca il protetto nessun toccherà, no,
no....

Rigoletto:
I am protected by the Duke, and no one
can touch me, no, no.....

Borsa, Marullo Conte di Ceprano::
pei tristi suoi modi di noi chi non ha?

Borsa, Marullo, Count Ceprano:
Who among you hasn't been the victim
of his vindictiveness?

Duca:
Ah sempre tu spingi lo scherzo
all'estremo....

Duke:
You always push your joking to
extremes....

Rigoletto:
Nessun, nessuno, nessun, nessuno.

Rigoletto:
No one, no one, no one, no one.
woe

Borsa, Marullo, Conte di Ceprano:
Vendetta! Vendetta!

Borsa, Marullo, Count Ceprano:
Vengeance! Vengeance!

Duca:
Quell'ira che sfidi, quell'ira che sfidi,
colpir ti potrà.

Duke:
The anger you have aroused will strike
back at you.

Rigoletto:
Nessun, nessuno del duca il protetto,
nessuno toccherà.

Rigoletto:
No one, I am protected by the Duke, and
no one can touch me.

Conte di Ceprano:
Vendetta! Sta notte chi ha core sia in armi
da me.

Count Ceprano:
Vengeance! Tonight those who have
courage bear arms with me.

Borsa, Marullo:
Vendetta! Sì! A notte sarà.

Borsa, Marullo:
Vengeance! Yes! It will be tonight.

Borsa, Marullo, Conte di Ceprano:
Sì vendetta!

Borsa, Marullo, Count Ceprano:
Yes vengeance!

Dancers from the other rooms enter the hall.

Duca, Rigoletto:
Tutto è gioja!

Duke, Rigoletto:
What entertainment!

Borsa, Marullo, Conte di Ceprano:
Sì vendetta! Sì, vendetta!
Sì, vendetta!

Borsa, Marullo, Count Ceprano:
Yes vengeance! Yes vengeance!
Yes vengeance!

Duca, Rigoletto:
Tutto è festa!

Duke, Rigoletto:
What entertainment!

Tutti:
Tutto è gioja, tutto è festa; tutto invitaci a
godere!
Oh guardate, non par questa or la reggia
del piacere!

All:
So much entertainment and amusement;
all the guests are enjoying themselves!
Look, nothing equals the extent of this
pleasure!

The voice of Count Monterone is heard from outside.

Monterone:
Ch'io gli parli.

Monterone:
I demand to speak to him.

Duca:
No!

Duke:
No!

Monterone:
Il voglio.

Monterone: *(as he enters)*
I demand it.

Borsa, Rigoletto, Marullo, Ceprano:
Monterone!

Borsa, Rigoletto, Marullo, Ceprano:
Monterone!

Monterone:
Sì, Monteron, la voce mia qual tuono vi
scuoterà dovunque.

Monterone: *(staring at the Duke)*
Yes, Monterone, the voice that makes you
shudder.

Rigoletto:
Ch'io gli parli.
Voi congiuraste, voi congiuraste contro
noi, signore; e noi, e noi, clementi in vero,
perdonammo
Qual vi piglia or delirio, a tutte l'ore di
vostra figlia a reclamar l'onore?

Rigoletto: *(mimicking Monterone)*
I demand to speak to him.
You have conspired, you have conspired
against us. And we, and we forgive you
with compassionate clemency.
What's the matter, are you still obsessed to
reclaim your daughter's honor?

Monterone:
Novello insulto!

Monterone: *(with contemptuous anger)*
Another insult!

Ah sì, a turbare, ah sì, a turbare sarò
vostr'orgie, verrò a gridare fino a che
vegga restarsi inulto di mia famiglia
l'atroce insulto; e se al carnefice pur mi
darete. spettro terribile mi rivedrete,
portante in mano il teschio mio, vendetta
a chiedere, vendetta a chiedere al mondo,
al mondo, a Dio.

Yes, I am tormented, tormented by your
debauchery. I have come to condemn the
atrocious insults you have perpetrated
against my family; and if you send me to
the executioner, my head will haunt you
like a horrible ghost. I ask for the world to
avenge me, and I ask vengeance from
God.

Duca:
Non più, arrestatelo!

Duke:
That's enough, arrest him!

Rigoletto:
È matto!

Borsa, Marullo, Conte di Ceprano:
Quai detti!

Monterone:
Ah, siate entrambi voi maledetti!

Slanciare il cane a leon morente è vile, o
Duca.

E tu, serpente, tu che d'un padre ridi al
dolore, sii maledetto!

Rigoletto:
(Che sento! Orrore!)

Duke, Borsa, Marullo, Ceprano:
Oh tu che la festa audace hai turbato, da
un genio d'inferno qui fosti guidato.

Rigoletto:
(Orrore!)

Duke, Borsa, Marullo, Ceprano:
È vano ogni detto, di qua t'allontana va,
trema, o vegliardo, dell'ira sovranna è
vano ogni detto, di qua t'allontana va,
trema, o vegliardo, dell'ira sovrana tu
l'hai provocata, più speme non v'è,
un'ora fatale fu questa per te, un'ora
fatale fu questa per te, fu questa per te.

Rigoletto:
He's mad!

Borsa, Marullo, Count Ceprano:
What impudence!

Monterone: *(to the Duke and Rigoletto)*
I curse both of you!

Duke, it is unconscionable to unleash this
vile dog at a dying lion.
(to Rigoletto)
And you, serpent, who mock a father's
agony, be accursed!

Rigoletto: *(stricken by terror)*
(What do I hear! What a horror!

Duke, Borsa, Marullo, Ceprano:
You have disturbed our amusement, your
audacious game has led us to Hell.

Rigoletto:
(What a horror!)

Duke, Borsa, Marullo, Ceprano:
Your words are hopeless. The curse
cannot be removed. Tremble, old man,
you have provoked the indignation of the
most holy.
There is no hope for you, a fatal destiny
has been ordained for you.

Monterone is led away by guards.
Rigoletto leaves in panic and terror.

| **Act I - Scene 2** |

A dark, deserted street at night.
There is a humble house with a small courtyard surrounded by a wall.
In the courtyard of the house there is a large tree and a garden seat.
In the wall a door leads to the street, and above the wall, a terrace supported by arches.
A door from the first floor opens to a terrace, from which there is a staircase.
From one side, the Ceprano palace is visible in the distance.

Rigoletto approaches his house, completely disguised by his cloak.
He is followed by a stranger: he is Sparafucile, an ominous looking man, wrapped in a
cloak from which the hilt of a sword projects.

Rigoletto:
(Quel vecchio maledivami!)

Rigoletto: *(muttering to himself)*
(That old man cursed me!

Andante mosso

Sparafucile:
Signor!

Sparafucile: *(nearing Rigoletto)*
Sir!

Rigoletto:
Va, non ho niente.

Rigoletto:
Go away, I have nothing.

Sparafucile:
Né il chiesi. A voi presente un uom di
spada sta.

Sparafucile:
That is not my reason. I present myself to
you as a man of the sword.

Rigoletto:
Un ladro?

Rigoletto:
A robber?

Sparafucile:
Un uom che libera per poco da un rivale,
e voi ne avete.

Sparafucile: *(mysteriously)*
A man who for very little money can rid
you of a rival, if you have the need.

Rigoletto:
Quale?

Rigoletto:
How?

Sparafucile:
La vostra donna è là.

Sparafucile:
Your woman is in there.

Rigolettto:
(Che sento!)
E quanto spendere per un signor dovrei?

Rigoletto:
(He knows my secret!)
How much does it cost to slay a noble?

Sparafucile:
Prezzo maggior vorrei.

Sparafucile:
I ask a high price for that.

Rigoletto:
Com'usasi pagar?

Rigoletto:
When must the price be paid?

Sparafucile:
Una metà s'anticipa, il resto si dà poi.

Sparafucile:
One half beforehand, the rest after the deed.

Rigoletto:
(Dimonio!)
E come puoi tanto securo oprar?

Rigoletto:
(What a demon!)
How sure are you of success?

Sparafucile:
Soglio in cittade uccidere, oppure nel mio
tetto. L'uomo di sera aspetto, una
stoccata, e muor.

Sparafucile:
I use my house, because it is dangerous to
kill in the city. I await the victim in the
evening; one thrust, and he is dead.

Rigoletto:
E come in casa?

Rigoletto:
How do you lure them to your house?

Sparafucile:
È facile, m'aiuta mia sorella, per le vie
danza è bella. Chi voglio attira, e allor.

Sparafucile:
It is easy. My sister helps me. She lures
them with her beauty and by dancing.

Rigoletto:
Comprendo.

Rigoletto:
I understand.

Sparafucile:
Senza strepito. È questo il mio stromento.
Vi serve?

Sparafucile: *(showing his sword)*
There is no noise. This is my instrument.
Can it serve you?

Rigoletto:
No, al momento.

Rigoletto:
No, not at the moment.

Sparafucile:
Peggio per voi.

Sparafucile:
You may regret it.

Rigoletto:
Chi sa?

Rigoletto:
Who knows?

Sparafucile:
Sparafucil mi nomino.

Rigoletto:
Straniero?

Sparafucile:
Borgognone.

Rigoletto:
E dove all'occasione?

Sparafucile:
Qui sempre a sera.

Rigoletto:
Va.

Sparafucile:
Sparafucil, Sparafucil.

Sparafucile:
My name is Sparafucil.

Rigoletto:
A foreigner?

Sparafucile: *(begins to depart)*
From Borgognone.

Rigoletto:
If I need you, where can I find you?

Sparafucile:
Here, every evening.

Rigoletto:
Go away.

Sparafucile: *(as he departs)*
Sparafucil, Sparafucil.

Rigoletto looks after Sparafucile intently.

Adagio
RIGOLETTO

Pa - ri   sia - mo!   io   la lin - gua,   egli ha il pugna - le.

Rigoletto:
Pari siamo! Io la lingua, egli ha il pugnale;
l'uomo son io che ride, ei quel che
spegne!
Quel vecchio maledivami!
O uomini! O natura!
Vil scellerato mi faceste voi!
Oh rabbia! Esser difforme!
Esser buffone!

Non dover, non poter altro che ridere!
Il retaggio d'ogni uom m'è tolto, il pianto!

Rigoletto:
We are the same! I use my tongue, he
uses the dagger; I am the man who
ridicules, and he is the one who kills!
That old man cursed me!
Oh world! Oh nature!
You made me wicked and evil!
What a fate! To be deformed!
To be a jester!

I am commanded to make others laugh!
I have inherited everyone's sorrows and
tears!

Questo padrone mio, giovin, giocondo, sì
possente, bello, sonnecchiando mi dice:
fa ch'io rida, buffone, forzarmi deggio, e
farlo!

My master, young, handsome, rich and
powerful, even commands me in his sleep:
Make me laugh, jester, and I must force
myself to obey him!

O, dannazione!
Odio a voi, cortigiani schernitori!
Quanta in mordervi ho gioia!
Se iniquo son, per cagion vostra è solo.
Ma in altr'uom qui mi cangio!

Oh damnation!
I hate you, contemptible courtiers!
My only joy is to taunt you!
If I am vile, it is because of you.
But in this house I am different!

Quel vecchio malediami!
Tal pensiero perché conturba ognor la
mente mia?
Mi coglierà sventura?
Ah no, è follia!

That old man cursed me!
Why does that thought keep agitating my
mind?
Is it an evil omen?
No, it is mere folly!

Rigoletto open the gate with a key, and then enters the courtyard.
Gilda rushes from the house and throws herself into her father's arms.

Allegro vivo

Rigoletto:
Figlia!

Rigoletto:
My daughter!

Gilda:
Mio padre!

Gilda:
My father!

Rigoletto:
A te dappresso trova sol gioia il core
oppresso.

Rigoletto:
To be near to you is my only joy; you
soothe my grieving heart.

Gilda:
Oh quanto amore!

Gilda:
Oh, you love me so much!

Rigoletto:
Mia vita sei! Senza te in terra qual bene
avrei?

Rigoletto:
You are my life! Without you, what
would I have in the world?

Gilda:
Voi sospirate! Che v'ange tanto?
Lo dite a questa povera figlia.
Se v'ha mistero per lei sia franto.
Ch'ella conosca la sua famiglia.

Gilda:
You are sighing! What troubles you?
Tell your poor daughter.
If something bothers you,
share it with you daughter.

Rigoletto:
Tu non ne hai.

Rigoletto:
You wouldn't understand it.

Gilda:
Qual nome avete?

Gilda:
What is your name?

Rigoletto:
A te che importa?

Rigoletto:
Is it that important to you?

Gilda:
Se non volete di voi parlarmi.

Gilda:
You don't wish to tell me.

Rigoletto:
Non uscir mai.

Rigoletto: *(interrupting Gilda)*
Don't ever leave the house.

Gilda:
Non vo' che al tempio.

Gilda:
Not even to go to church.

Rigoletto:
Or ben tu fai.

Rigoletto:
That is all right.

Gilda:
Se non di voi, almen chi sia fate ch'io
sappia la madre mia.

Gilda:
Perhaps at least you can tell me about my
mother.

Andante
RIGOLETTO

Deh non parla-re al mi-se-ro   *del suo   perdu-to   be   -   ne.*

Rigoletto:
Deh non parlare al misero del suo perduto
bene
Ella sentia, quell'angelo, pietà delle mie
pene.
Solo, difforme, povero, per compassion
mi amò.
Ah! Moria, moria, le zolle coprano lievi
quel capo amato.
Sola or tu resti al misero.
Dio, sii ringraziato!

Rigoletto:
Don't speak of my grief since I lost that
love.
That angel felt pity for my anguish and
sorrows.
She loved me compassionately, a man
who was alone, deformed, and poor.
She is dead, covered by earth, her soul
raised to Heaven.
Only you remain from that sorrow.
God, may I thank you for that!

Gilda:
Quanto dolor!
Che spremere sì amaro pianto può?
Padre, non più, calmatevi.
Mi lacera tal vista.
Il nome vostro ditemi, il duol che sì
v'attrista.

Rigoletto:
A che nomarmi? È inutile!
Padre ti sono, e basti.
Me forse al mondo temono, d'alcuno ho
forse gli asti.
Altri mi maledicono.

Gilda:
Patria, parenti, amici, voi dunque non
avete?

Rigoletto:
Patria! Parenti! Dici?
Culto, famiglia, patria, il mio universo è
in te!

Gilda:
Ah se può lieto rendervi, gioia è la vita a
me!

Già da tre lune son qui venuta, né la
cittade ho ancor veduta; se il concedete,
farlo or potrei.

Rigoletto:
Mai, Mai! Uscita, dimmi unqua sei?

Gilda:
No.

Rigoletto:
Guai!

Gilda:
(Ah! Che dissi!)

Gilda: *(sobbing)*
What suffering!
How that love has moved you to tears?
Father, no more, calm yourself.
Your look upsets me.
Tell me your name, and the distress that
has saddened you.

Rigoletto:
What is my name? It is unnecessary!
I am father, and that is enough.
In the world, there are some who fear me,
and some who hate me.
Others curse me.

Gilda:
Then you do not have a homeland,
relatives, or friends?

Rigoletto:
Homeland! Relatives! What do you say?
My soul, family, country, my entire
universe is you!

Gilda:
Whatever makes you happy, gives me joy
and happiness!

But we've already here three months, and
I haven't seen the city yet. I'd like to be
able to, if you would let me.

Rigoletto:
Never, never! Have you gone out?

Gilda:
No.

Rigoletto:
It would be disastrous!

Gilda:
(Oh, what I have said!)

Rigoletto:
Ben te ne guarda!
(Potrien seguirla, rapirla ancora! Qui d'un
buffone si disonora la figlia, e se ne ride.
Orror!)

Rigoletto:
Obey me!
(They would follow her and rape her, and
laugh as they dishonored the daughter of
a jester. What a horror!)

Rigoletto rushes towards the house and calls Giovanna, Gilda's nurse.

Olà?   Can you come out?

Giovanna:
Signor!

Giovanna:
Sir!

Rigoletto:
Venendo, mi vede alcuno?
Bada, di' il vero.

Rigoletto:
Has anyone seen me coming here?
Tell me the truth.

Giovanna:
Ah no, nessuno.

Giovanna:
No, no one.

Rigoletto:
Sta ben. La porta che dà al bastione è
sempre chiusa?

Rigoletto:
Very well. Has the door from the terrace
always remained closed?

Giovanna:
Ognor si sta.

Giovanna:
Always closed.

Allegro moderato assai
RIGOLETTO

Ah! Veglia o don - na, questo fio-re che a te pur - ro confi- dai.

Rigoletto:
Ah! Veglia, o donna, questo fiore che a te
puro confidai; veglia attenta, e non sia
mai che s'offuschi il suo candor.
Tu dei venti dal furore ch 'altri fiori
hanno piegato lo difendi, e immacolato lo
ridona al genitor.

Rigoletto: *(to Giovanna)*
Lady, guard this innocent flower who I
place in your trust; watch her carefully,
and don't let her purity ever be darkened.
In threatening storms other flowers have
yielded their defense, and returned a
daughter to a father in disgrace.

Gilda:
Quanto affetto! Quali cure!
Che temete, padre mio?

Gilda:
So much love! So much concern!
Father, why are you so fearful?

Lassù in cielo, presso Dio veglia un
angiol protettor. Da noi stoglie le sventure
di mia madre il priego santo; non fia mai
divelto o infranto questo a voi diletto fior.

Up there in Heaven, close to God, is my
mother, an angel protecting us from
misfortune; she protects your treasured
flower.

Meanwhile, the Duke, dressed in ordinary street clothes,
appears outside Rigoletto's house.

Rigoletto:
Alcuno è fuori.

Rigoletto: *(hearing noise)*
Someone is out there.

Rigoletto opens the courtyard door and goes out to investigate the noise.
The Duke evades him, enters the courtyard, and hides behind a tree.
He throws a purse to Giovanna, and makes a sign that she be silent.

Gilda:
Cielo! Sempre novel sospetto.

Gilda:
Heavens! Always new suspicions.

Rigoletto:
Alla chiesa vi seguiva mai nessuno?

Rigoletto: *(questioning Giovanna)*
Did anyone follow you from church?

Giovanna:
Mai.

Giovanna:
No one.

Duca:
(Rigoletto!)

Duke: *(from hiding)*
(Rigoletto!)

Rigoletto:
Se talor qui picchiano guardatevi da aprir.

Rigoletto:
If someone knocks, be cautious in
opening the gate.

Giovanna:
Nemmeno al duca.

Giovanna:
Not even for the Duke.

Rigoletto:
Meno che a tutti a lui.
Mia figlia addio.

Rigoletto:
Least of all him.
Farewell my daughter.

Duca:
(Sua figlia!)

Duke:
(His daughter!)

Gilda:
Addio, mio padre.

Gilda:
Farewell, my father.

Rigoletto embraces Gilda, and then departs, carefully closing the door behind him.

Gilda:
Giovanna, ho dei rimorsi.

Gilda:
Giovanna, I feel so guilty.

Giovanna:
E perché mai?

Giovanna:
And why?

Gilda:
Tacqui che un giovin ne seguiva al
tempio.

Gilda:
I didn't tell him that a young man
followed me home from church.

Giovanna:
Perché ciò dirgli?
L'odiate dunque cotesto giovin, voi?

Giovanna:
Why was it necessary to tell him?
Do you want to chase the young man away?

Gilda:
No, no, ché troppo è bello e spira amore.

Gilda:
No, he's so handsome and inspires love.

Giovanna:
E magnanimo sembra e gran signore.

Giovanna:
He seems to be so generous and noble.

Gilda:
Signor né principe, io lo vorrei;
sento che povero, più l'amerei.
Sognando o vigile sempre lo chiamo,
e l'alma in estasi gli dice t'a...

Gilda:
He's not a prince, although I would wish it;
I love him more because he's poor.
I always call him in my dreams,
and my ecstatic soul tells him I love...

The Duke emerges from hiding, signals Giovanna to leave.
Then he kneels before Gilda.

Duca:
T'amo! T'amo ripetilo,
sì caro accento, un puro schiudimi ciel di
contento!

Duke:
I love you! I love you and I repeat it,
a beloved sound, that opens the bliss of
the Heavens!

Gilda:
Giovanna? Ahi misera!
Non v'è più alcuno che qui rispondami!
Oh Dio! Nessuno!

Gilda: *(surprised and fearful)*
Giovanna? How frightful!
There's no one here to answer me!
Oh God! No one!

Duca:
Son io coll'anima che ti rispondo.
Ah due che s'amano son tutto un mondo!

Duke:
It is I whose soul answers you.
Two people who love each other is all
there is in the entire world!

Gilda:
Chi mai, chi giungere vi fece a me?

Gilda:
Who made you come here?

Duca:
Se angelo o demone, che importa a te?
Io t'amo.

Duke:
Angel or demon, is it important to you?
I love you.

Gilda:
Uscitene.

Gilda:
Leave me.

Duca:
Uscire! Adesso!
Ora che accendene un fuoco istesso!
Ah inseparabile d'amore il dio stringeva,
o vergine, tuo fato al mio!

Duke:
Leave! Right now!
Now that the fire has been kindled!
Innocent maiden, we are possessed by an
inseparable love. Your fate is to be mine!

Andantino
DUKE

È il sol dell 'anima, la vita è a-more sua vo - ce è il palpito del nos-tro   core.

È il sol dell'anima, la vita è amore, sua
voce è il palpito del nostro core.
E fama e gloria, potenza e trono, umane,
fragili qui cose sono:
una pur avvene, sola, divina, é amor che
agli angeli, agli angeli più ne avvicina!

Life is love, the sun of the soul, its voice
the throb of our hearts.
Fame and glory, power and throne,
humanity, are unimportant here:
one future, ours, divine, is love that even
the angels cannot approach!

Adunque amiamoci, donna celeste,
d'invidia agli uomini, sarò per te.

Therefore we love each other, celestial
woman, envy of men, and I will be yours.

Gilda:
Ah de' miei vergini sogni son queste le
voci tenere, sì care a me!

Gilda:
That tender voice is from my sublime
dreams. Yes, you are dear to me!

Duca:
Che m'ami, deh! Ripetimi.

Duke:
Repeat to me that you love me!

Gilda:
L'udiste.

Gilda:
Listen to it.

Duca:
Oh me felice!

Duke:
You make me so happy!

Gilda:
Il nome vostro ditemi; saperlo non mi
lice?

Gilda:
Tell me your name. Would I forget it if I
knew it?

Ceprano:
(Il loco è qui.)

Ceprano: *(in the street)*
(This is the place.)

Duca:
Mi nomino.

Duke: *(thinking with seriousness)*
My name.

Borsa:
Sta ben.

Borsa: *(to Ceprano)*
Very well.

Duca:
Gualtier Maldè. Studente sono, e povero.

Duke:
Walter Maldè. I am a poor student.

Giovanna:
Rumor di passi è fuore.

Giovanna: *(returning in agitation)*
There's the noise of footsteps outside.

Gilda:
Forse mio padre.

Gilda:
Perhaps it is my father.

Duca:
(Ah cogliere potessi il traditore che sì mi
sturba!)

Duke:
(If I could only find the traitor who has
thwarted my adventure!)

Gilda:
Adducilo di qua al bastione or ite.

Gilda: *(to Giovanna)*
Let him leave by the terrace door.

Duca:
Di' m'amerai tu?

Duke:
Tell me, do you love me?

Gilda:
E voi?

Gilda:
And you?

Duca:
L'intera vita, poi.

Duke:
Eternally.

Duca e Gilda:
Non più, non più, partite.

Duke and Gilda:
No more, leave.

Vivacissimo
DUKE

Ad - di - o   ad - di - o   spe - ran - za ed anima.

Addio, addio, speranza ed anima sol tu sarai per me.
Addio, addio, vivrà immutabile l'affetto mio per te.

Farewell, farewell, you alone are my hope and soul.
Farewell, farewell, our love will be constant. I will live only for you.

Giovanna escorts the Duke into the house.
Gilda remains, gazing at him blissfully as he leaves.

Gilda:
Gualtier Maldè! Nome di lui sì amato, scolpisciti nel core innamorato!

Gilda:
Walter Maldè! The name of my lover is carved in my enchanted heart!

Allegro moderato
GILDA

Ca-ro no-me che il mio cor   fe - sti pri - mo pal - pi - tar.

Caro nome che il mio cor
festi primo palpitar,
le delizie dell'amor
mi dêi sempre rammentar!

Dearest name, the first love
to throb in my heart,
I will always remember the delights of
love that you have brought to me!

Col pensiero il mio desir a te sempre
ognora volerà,
e pur l'ultimo sospir,
caro nome, tuo sarà!

My thoughts and desires
will always be with you,
and if it is my last sigh,
dear name, it will always be yours!

Gilda enters the house, and then reappears on the terrace,
rapturously watching her lover disappear into the night.

Borsa:
È là.

Borsa: *(pointing to Gilda)*
There she is.

Ceprano:
Miratela.

Ceprano:
Look at her.

Cortigiani:.
Oh quanto è bella!

Courtiers:
Look how beautiful she is!

Marullo:
Par fata od angiol.

Marullo:
Like a fairy or an angel.

Cortigiani:
L'amante è quella di Rigoletto!

Courtiers:
That woman is Rigoletto's lover!

Rigoletto appears.

Rigoletto:
(Riedo! Perché?)

Rigoletto: *(upon seeing the courtiers)*
(What can this mean?)

Borsa:
Silenzio, all'opra, badate a me.

Borsa: *(to the courtiers)*
Quiet, there's work to do, listen to me.

Rigoletto:
(Ah da quel vecchio fui maledetto!)

Rigoletto:
(It was that curse from that old man!)

Rigoletto runs into Borsa.

Chi è là?

Who's there?

Borsa:
Tacete, c'è Rigoletto.

Borsa: *(to the courtiers)*
Quiet, there's Rigoletto.

Ceprano:
Vittoria doppia! L'uccideremo.

Ceprano:
A double triumph! Let's kill him.

Borsa:
No, ché domani più rideremo.

Borsa:
No, because we want to laugh tomorrow.

Marullo:
Or tutto aggiusto.

Marullo:
Let's make peace with him.

Rigoletto:
Chi parla qua?

Rigoletto:
Who's talking over there?

Marullo:
Ehi Rigoletto? Di'!

Marullo:
Hey Rigoletto? Speak!

Rigoletto:
Chi va là?

Rigoletto: *(in an angry voice)*
Who goes there?

Marullo:
Eh non mangiarci! Son...

Marullo:
Don't be so irritable! We are...

Rigoletto:
Chi?

Rigoletto:
Who?

Marullo:
Marullo.

Rigoletto:
In tanto bujo lo sguardo è nullo.

Marullo:
Qui ne condusse ridevol cosa, torre a
Ceprano vogliam la sposa.

Rigoletto:
(Ohimè respiro!)
Ma come entrare?

Marullo:
La vostra chiave?

Non dubitare. Non dee mancarci lo
stratagemma.

Marullo:
Marullo.

Rigoletto:
It's hard to see in such darkness.

Marullo:
We're here to have some fun. We want to
abduct Ceprano's wife.

Rigoletto: _(expressing relief)_
(I can breathe again!)
How can you enter the house?

Marullo: _(aside to Ceprano)_
Where's your key?
(aside to Rigoletto)
Don't worry. Every detail has been
planned.

Marullo gives the key to Rigoletto.

Ecco le chiavi.

Here's the key.

Rigoletto:
Sento il tuo stemma.
(Ah terror vano fu dunque il mio!)
N'è là il palazzo, con voi son 'io.

Marullo:
Siam mascherati.

Rigoletto:
Ch'io pur mi mascheri a me una larva?

Marullo:
Sì, pronta è già.Terrai la scala.

Rigoletto:
I can feel it's crest.
(It was just me, my unnecessary fears!)
She's there in the palace, I'm with you.

Marullo:
We are masked.

Rigoletto:
It's so dark, do I need a mask too?

Marullo:
Yes, we're ready. Hold the ladder.

Marullo masks Rigoletto, and binds a handkerchief over his eyes.
Rigoletto, unaware of where he is, holds the ladder beneath the terrace of his own house.

Rigoletto:
Fitta è la tenebra.

Marullo:
La benda cieco e sordo il fa.

Rigoletto:
It's so dark.

Marullo: _(to the courtiers)_
With the mask, he's both deaf and blind.

Some courtiers ascend the terrace and break open the door.
They descend to the lower floor and open the door for the other courtiers.

Tutti:
Zitti, zitti moviamo a vendetta,
ne sia colto or che meno l'aspetta.
Derisore sì audace costante a sua volta
schernito sarà!
Cheti, cheti, rubiamgli l'amante,
e la corte doman riderà.

All:
Quietly, we achieve our vengeance,
without a word or even a sound.
We will scorn the man for his incessant,
audacious mockery!
Swiftly, cautiously, we'll abduct his lover,
and tomorrow the court will ridicule him.

Some courtiers exit the house carrying Gilda, who has been blindfolded with a
handkerchief. As they escape with her, she drops her scarf.

Gilda:
Soccorso, padre mio!

Gilda: *(from the distance)*
Father, help me!

Cortigiani:
Vittoria!

Courtiers:
Victory!

Gilda:
Aita!

Gilda: *(from further away)*
Help me!

Rigoletto:
Non han finito ancor!
Qual derisione!

Rigoletto:
They haven't finished yet!
What jesting!

Rigoletto places his hands to his eyes.

Sono bendato!

My eyes are bandaged!

Rigoletto tears off the bandage and mask.
He picks up a lantern left by one of the courtiers,
and recognizes Gilda's scarf on the ground.
He rushes into the house and returns dragging Giovanna.
He stares at her in bewilderment, tries to express his agony, but he cannot.
He realizes that Gilda has been abducted; in anguish,
he attributes the horrible event to Monterone's curse.

Ah!Ah! Ah! La maledizione!

Ah! Ah!Ah! The curse!

Act II

*An hall in the Duke's palace. The doors to the Duke's bedroom are closed.
On each side of the doors there is a portrait respectively of the Duke and the Duchess.
The Duke enters the in great agitation.*

Duca:
Ella mi fu rapita!
E quando, o ciel?
Ne'brevi istanti, prima che il mio presagio
interno sull'orma corsa ancora mi
spingesse!

Schiuso era l'uscio!
E la magion deserta!
E dove ora sarà quell'angiol caro?
Colei che prima potè in questo core destar
la fiamma di costanti affetti?

Colei sì pura, al cui modesto sguardo
quasi spinto a virtù talor mi credo!
Ella mi fu rapita!
E chi l'ardiva?
Ma ne avrò vendetta, lo chiede il pianto
della mia diletta.

Duke:
She has overwhelmed me!
Heaven, when did this happen to me?
All of a sudden, I could not rest, and in
my anxiety, I was compelled to return to
her!

The doors of the house were open!
And the house was deserted!
And where was my dear angel?
Why has she seduced my heart and
awakened flames of love?

She is indeed pure and virtuous, and has
such a charming glance!
She has overwhelmed me!
And who would dare to abduct her?
But I will have revenge, and seek to dry
the tears of my beloved.

Adagio
DUKE

Par - mi   veder le la - grime   scorren - ti da quel cig-lio,

Parmi veder le lagrime scorrenti da quel
ciglio, quando fra il dubbio e l'ansia del
subito periglio, dell'amor nostro memore,
il suo Gualtier chiamò.

Ned ei potea soccorrerti, cara fanciulla
amata, ei che vorria coll'anima farti
quaggiù beata; ei che le sfere agli angeli,
per te non invidiò.

I seem to see tears running from those
eyes, calling in doubt and anxiety from
her sudden danger. Your Walter
remembers our love and calls to you.

If I could help you, dearest love, and with
all my soul make you blessed here; I
would not envy you in the realm of the
angels.

Marullo, Borsa, Ceprano and courtiers enter the hall in agitation.

Borsa, Marullo, Ceprano:
Duca, duca!

Borsa, Marullo, Ceprano:
Duke, Duke!

Duca:
Ebben?

Duke:
What is the news?

Borsa, Marullo, Ceprano:
L'amante fu rapita a Rigoletto.

Borsa, Marullo, Ceprano:
We have seized Rigoletto's lover!

Duca:
Come? E donde?

Duke:
How? Where is she?

Borsa, Marullo, Ceprano:
Dal suo tetto.

Borsa, Marullo, Ceprano:
From her home.

Duca:
Ah, ah! Dite, come fu?

Duke:
Oh! Tell me, how did it happen?

Borsa, Marullo, Ceprano:
Scorrendo uniti remota via, brev'ora dopo
caduto il dì, come previsto ben s'era in
pria, rara beltà ci si scoprì.

Era l'amante di Rigoletto, che, vista
appena, si dileguò.
Già di rapirla s'avea il progetto,quando il
buffone ver noi spuntò;
che di Ceprano noi la contessa rapir
volessimo, stolto credé;
la scala, quindi, all'uopo messa, bendato,
ei stesso ferma tenè.
Salimmo, e rapidi la giovinetta a noi
riusciva quindi asportar.
Quand'ei s'accorse della vendettarestò
scornato ad imprecar, ad imprecar.

Borsa, Marullo, Ceprano:
It was dusk, and we were all together in a
remote street. Like a vision out of the
shadows, we discovered this rare beauty.

She was Rigoletto's lover. We saw for an
instant, and then she vanished.
We decided to abduct her, but Rigoletto
saw us and interrupted us;
so we told him we wanted to abduct
Countess Ceprano. He believed the lie;
we had him hold the ladder, we bandaged
his eyes, and he obliged us.
We rapidly went upstairs, grabbed her and
immediately left.
When he discovered our revenge, he
condemned and cursed us.

Duca:
(Cielo! È dessa! La mia diletta!)

Ma dove or trovasi la poveretta?

Duke: *(to himself)*
Heavens! It is she! My adored one!
(to the courtiers)
Where can I find the poor girl?

Borsa, Marullo, Ceprano:
Fu da noi stessi addotta or qui.

Borsa, Marullo, Ceprano:
We've brought her here.

Duca:
(Ah, tutto il ciel non mi rapì!)

Possente amor mi chiama, volar io deggio
a lei; il serto mio darei per consolar quel
cor.
Ah! Sappia alfin chi l'ama, conosca alfin
chi sono, apprenda ch'anco in trono ha
degli schiavi Amor.

Borsa, Marullo, Ceprano:
Oh qual pensier or l'agita, come cangiò
d'umor!

Duke: *(becoming joyful at the news)*
(Heaven has not deceived me!)

The [power of love calls me. I must
possess you; I would give my crown to
console that heart.
Finally she will know it is that loves her,
she will know who I am, that the crown is
a slave of Love.

Borsa, Marullo, Ceprano:
Look how his agitation has suddenly
changed to happiness!

The Duke rushes to his bedroom.
Rigoletto is heard from outside.

Marullo:
Povero Rigoletto!

Marullo:
Poor Rigoletto!

Rigoletto:
La rà, la rà, la la, la rà, la rà, la rà, la rà la
rà, la la, la rà, la rà.

Rigoletto:
La ra, la ra, la la, la ra, la ra, la ra, la ra la
ra, la la, la ra, la ra.

Tutti:
Ei vien! Silenzio.

All:
Here he comes! Quiet.

Rigoletto enters the hall, nonchalant and pretending indifference.

Borsa, Marullo, Ceprano:
Oh buon giorno, Rigoletto.

Borsa, Marullo, Ceprano:
Good morning, Rigoletto.

Rigoletto:
(Han tutti fatto il colpo!)

Rigoletto:
(They're all conspirators!)

Ceprano:
Ch'hai di nuovo, buffon?

Ceprano:
What's new, jester?

Rigoletto:
Ch'hai di nuovo, buffon?
Che dell'usato più noioso voi siete.

Rigoletto: *(imitating Ceprano)*
What's new, jester?
You seem unusually annoyed.

Borsa, Marullo, Ceprano:
Ah! Ah! Ah!

Borsa, Marullo, Ceprano: *(laughing)*
Hah! Hah! Hah!

Rigoletto:
La rà, la rà, la la la rà, la rà, la rà, la rà.

(Ove l'avran nascosta?)

Borsa, Marullo, Ceprano:
(Guardate com'è inquieto!)

Rigoletto:
La rà, la rà, la rà, la rà, la rà, la rà, la rà, la
rà, la rà, la rà, la rà.

Borsa, Marullo, Ceprano:
Sì! Sì! Guardate com'è inquieto!

Rigoletto:
Son felice che nulla a voi nuocesse l'aria
di questa notte.

Marullo:
Questa notte!

Rigoletto:
Sì. Oh fu il bel colpo!

Marullo:
S'ho dormito sempre!

Rigoletto:
Ah, voi dormiste! Avrò dunque sognato!

Rigoletto finds a handkerchief and seizes it.

La rà, la rà, la la, la rà, la rà, la rà, la la.

Borsa, Marullo, Ceprano:
(Ve', come tutto osserva!)

Rigoletto:
(Non è il suo.)
Dorme il Duca tuttor?

Borsa, Marullo, Ceprano:
Sì, dorme ancora.

Rigoletto: *(wandering inquisitively)*
La ra, la ra, la la la ra, la ra, la ra, la ra.

(Where could they have hidden her?)

Borsa, Marullo, Ceprano:
(Look at how agitated he is!)

Rigoletto:
La ra, la ra, la la, la ra, la ra, la ra, la ra la
ra, la la, la ra, la ra.

Borsa, Marullo, Ceprano:
Yes! Yes! Look how agitated he is!

Rigoletto: *(to Marullo)*
I'm pleased that none of you were
harmed by this evening's air.

Marullo:
This evening!

Rigoletto:
Yes, it was quite a good joke!

Marullo:
I have never slept better!

Rigoletto:
You slept! I wish I could have slept!

La ra, la ra, la la, la ra, la ra, la ra, la la.

Borsa, Marullo, Ceprano:
(Look at how he scrutinizes everything!)

Rigoletto: *(looking at the handkerchief)*
(It's not hers.)
Is the Duke still sleeping?

Borsa, Marullo, Ceprano:
Yes, he's still sleeping.

Paggio:
Al suo sposo parlar vuol la Duchessa.

Page:
The Duchess wishes to speak to her husband.

Ceprano:
Dorme.

Ceprano:
He's sleeping.

Paggio:
Qui or or con voi non era?

Page:
Wasn't he here with you just before?

Borsa:
È a caccia

Borsa:
He's hunting.

Paggio:
Senza paggi! Senz'armi!

Page:
Without pages! Without weapons!

Borsa, Marullo, Ceprano:
E non capisci che per ora vedere non può alcuno?

Borsa, Marullo, Ceprano:
Don't you understand that he doesn't want to see anyone now?

Rigoletto:
Ah! Ella è qui dunque!
Ella è col Duca!

Rigoletto:
She is with him!
She is with the Duke!

Borsa, Marullo, Ceprano:
Chi?

Borsa, Marullo, Ceprano:
Who?

Rigoletto:
La giovin che sta notte al mio tetto rapiste.
Ma la saprò riprender. Ella è là.

Rigoletto:
The young girl you abducted from my house this evening.
I know I can recover her. She is there.

Borsa, Marullo, Ceprano:
Se l'amante perdesti, la ricerca altrove.

Borsa, Marullo, Ceprano:
If you lost your lover, find her elsewhere.

Rigoletto:
Io vo' mia figlia.

Rigoletto:
I want my daughter.

Borsa, Marullo, Ceprano:
La sua figlia!

Borsa, Marullo, Ceprano:
His daughter!

Rigoletto:
Sì, la mia figlia.
D'una tal vittoria che?
Adesso non ridete?
Ella è là! La vogl'io la renderete!

Rigoletto:
Yes, my daughter.
What kind of victory is that?
You're not laughing now?
She is there! I want you to return her!

Andante mosso agitato
RIGOLETTO

Cor-ti -giani,   vil razza   da-nnata,   per qual prezzo vendeste il mio cor?

Cortigiani, vil razza dannata, per qual
prezzo vendeste il mio bene?
A voi nulla per l'oro sconviene!

Ma mia figlia è impagabil tesor.
La rendete o, se pur disarmata, questa
man per voi fora cruenta;
nulla in terra più l'uomo paventa, se dei
figli difende l'onor.

Quella porta, assassini, assassini,
m'aprite, la porta, la porta, assassini,
m'aprite.

Ah! Voi tutti a me contro venite!
Tutti contra me!
Ah! Ebben, piango, Marullo, signore, tu
ch'hai l'alma gentil come il core, dimmi
tu dove l'hanno nascosta?
È là? Non è vero?
Tu taci! Ohimè!

Miei signori, perdono, pietate, al
vegliardo la figlia ridate.
Ridonarla a voi nulla ora costa, tutto al
mondo è tal figlia per me.
Pietà, pietà, signori!

Courtiers, damned vile race, for what
price have you sold my treasure?
For you, there is no longer decency!

But my daughter is a priceless treasure.
Return her, or be defenseless against this
hand that will pierce your skull;
nothing on earth is more frightening than
a father defending his daughter's honor.

That door, assassins, assassins,
open it, the door, the door, assassins, open
it.

Ah! You're all against me!
All against me!
Well, I am crying. Marullo, sir, you have a
gentle soul like your heart, tell me where
you have hidden her?
Is she there? Is that true?
You are quiet! How unfortunate!

My lords, pardon, pity, and return the
daughter of an old man.
Return her, it costs you nothing, my
daughter is everything in the world to me.
Mercy, my lords!

Gilda rushes from the room and throws herself in her father's arms.

Gilda:
Mio padre!

Gilda:
Father!

Rigoletto:
Dio! Mia Gilda! Signori in essa è tutta la
mia famiglia.

Rigoletto:
God! My Gilda! Lords, in this girl you see
my entire family.

Non temer più nulla, angelo mio fu
scherzo! Non è vero?

Don't fear anything, my angel, it was all a
joke! Isn't that true?

Io che pur piansi or rido.
E tu a che piangi?

I was weeping, but now I rejoice.
And why are you crying?

Gilda:
Ah l'onta, padre mio.

Gilda:
Father, I was dishonored.

Rigoletto:
Cielo! Che dici?

Rigoletto:
Heavens! What did you say?

Gilda:
Arrosir voglio innanzi a voi soltanto.

Gilda:
I want to blush, and be alone with you.

Rigoletto:
Ite di qua, voi tutti.
Se il duca vostro d'appressarsi osasse,
ch'ei non entri, gli dite, e ch'io ci sono.

Rigoletto: *(imperiously to the courtiers)*
All of you leave.
If the Duke dares to approach us, tell him
to stay away.

Courtiers:
(Coi fanciulli e co'dementi spesso giova il
simular. Partiam pur, ma quel ch'ei tenti
non lasciamo d'osservar.)

Courtiers:
(We cannot pretend to help insane men
with their children. Let's leave, we don't
want to observe his agony.)

The courtiers exit, leaving Rigoletto and Gilda alone.

Rigoletto:
Parla, siam soli.

Rigoletto:
Speak to me, we're alone.

Gilda:
(Ciel! Dammi coraggio!)

Gilda:
(Heaven! Give me courage!)

Andantino
GILDA

Tutte le fe - ste al tem - pio   *mentre prega - va Id - dio,*

Tutte le feste al tempio mentre pregava
Iddio, bello e fatale un giovine offriasi al
guardo mio, se i labbri nostri tacquero,
dagl'occhi il cor, il cor parlò.

At the festivals at church, while I was
praying to God, a handsome and
irresistible man offered to protect me, our
lips could not utter what was in our
hearts.

Furtivo fra le tenebre sol ieri a me
giungeva. Sono studente, povero,
commosso mi diceva, e con ardente
palpito amor mi protestò.

Yesterday, as evening fell, he stood before
me. He told me he was a poor student,
and ardently declared his love for me.

Partì, il mio core aprivasi a speme più
gradita, quando improvvisi apparvero
color che m'han rapita, e a forza qui
m'addussero nell'ansia più crudel.

After he left, my heart became stirred by
profound hope. Then in the darkness they
abducted me, and brought me by force to
experience this cruel anguish.

Rigoletto:
Ah! (Solo per me l'infamia a te chiedeva,
o Dio, ch'ella potesse ascendere quanto
caduto er'io.
Ah! Presso del patibolo bisogna ben
l'altare!
Ma tutto ora scompare, l'altare, si
rovesciò!)

Rigoletto: *(to himself)*
Ah! (I prayed to God that I might avoid
this disgrace, that she would be able to
avoid the evil that has fallen on me.
Ah! An altar is needed next to the
executioner's scaffold!
But all has disappeared, the altar, it has
been turned back!)

(to Gilda)
Piangi! Piangi fanciulla, fanciulla piangi,
scorrer, scorrer fà il pianto sul mio cor.

(to Gilda)
Cry! Cry child, child cry,
your tears are flowing in my heart.

Gilda:
Padre, in voi parla un angel per me
consolator.

Gilda:
Father, a consoling angel speaks from
your voice.

Rigoletto:
Compiuto pur quanto a fare mi resta,
lasciare potremo quest'aura funesta.

Rigoletto:
What remains for us is to leave this
sinister place.

Gilda:
Sì.

Gilda:
Yes.

Rigoletto:
(E tutto un sol giorno cangiare potè!)

Rigoletto: *(to himself)*
(And all in one day our fate has changed!)

Monterone, escorted by armed guards, passes through the hall.

Usciere:
Schiudete, ire al carcere Monteron dee.

Ushers:
Open up, so Monterone can go to his cell.

Monterone stops before the portrait of the Duke.

Monterone:
Poichè fosti invano da me maledetto, nè
un fulmine o un ferro colpiva il tuo petto,
felice pur anco, o duca, vivrai!

Monterone:
So my curse has been in vain, neither a
thunderbolt or steel has entered your
breast. Duke, you are still live happily!

Monterone is led away by the guards.

Rigoletto:
No, vecchio t'inganni,
un vindice avrai!

Rigoletto:
No, old man, you are mistaken, you will
yet have vengeance!

Rigoletto:

Rigoletto: *(addressing the Duke's portrait)*

Allegro vivo
RIGOLETTO

Sì,   ven - det - ta, tre-men - da ven - det - ta,

Sì, vendetta, tremenda vendetta di
quest'anima è solo desio, di punirti già
l'ora s'affretta, che fatale per te tuonerà.
Come fulmin scagliato da Dio, te colpire
il buffone saprà.

Yes, a frightful vengeance is all that this
soul desires, the fatal thunder of your
punishment will arrive quickly.
Like a thunderbolt from God, you will
know that the blow came from the jester.

Gilda:
O mio padre, qual gioia feroce balenarvi
ne gl'occhi vegg'io!
Perdonate, a noi pure una voce di
perdono dal cielo verrà.
(Mi tradiva, pur l'amo, gran Dio!
Per l'ingrato ti chiedo pietà!)

Gilda:
My father, what ferocious joy flashes
from you old eyes!
Pardon him. Let a pure voice from
Heaven grant him forgiveness!
(He betrayed me, but I love him!
Oh God, I beg forgiveness for the wicked
man!)

Rigoletto and Gilda exit.

ACT III

The shore of the Mincio River. There is a two-story house: a rustic Inn.

It is night. Gilda and Rigoletto are outside the house; inside, Sparafucile is seated at a table, polishing his belt, and unaware that Rigoletto and Gilda are outside.

Rigoletto:
E l'ami?

Rigoletto:
Do you still love him?

Gilda:
Sempre.

Gilda:
Always.

Rigoletto:
Pure tempo a guarirne t'ho lasciato.

Rigoletto:
I have left you enough time to cure
yourself of this infatuation.

Gilda:
Io l'amo.

Gilda:
I love him.

Rigoletto:
Povero cor di donna! Ah il vile infame!
Ma ne avrai vendetta, o Gilda!

Rigoletto:
A poor woman's heart! That vile traitor!
But Gilda you will yet have revenge!

Gilda:
Pietà, mio padre!

Gilda:
Father, have mercy!

Rigoletto:
E se tu certa fossi ch'ei ti tradisse,
l'ameresti ancora?

Rigoletto:
If I could convince you that he betrayed
you, would you still love him?

Gilda:
Nol so, ma pur m'adora.

Gilda:
I don't know, but he indeed adores me.

Rigoletto:
Egli?

Rigoletto:
He does?

Gilda:
Sì.

Gilda:
Yes.

Rigoletto leads Gilda to the house where they can spy inside.

Rigoletto:
Ebben, osserva dunque.

Rigoletto:
Well, then observe inside.

Gilda:
Un uomo vedo.

Gilda:
I see a man.

Rigoletto:
Per poco attendi.

Rigoletto:
Watch him attentively.

The Duke, disguised as a cavalry officer, is seen inside the Inn.

Gilda:
Ah padre mio!

Gilda: *(startled)*
Oh, father!

Duca:
Due cose, e tosto.

Duke: *(to Sparafucile)*
Two things, right away.

Sparafucile:
Quali?

Sparafucile:
What are they?

Duca:
Una stanza e del vino.

Duke:
A room and wine.

Rigoletto:
(Son questi i suoi costumi!)

Rigoletto:
(Those are his usual adventures!)

Sparafucile:
(Oh il bel zerbino!)

Sparafucile:
(Oh what a dandy!)

Allegretto
DUKE

La donna è mobile qual piuma al vento, muta d'ac-cen - to   e di pen-si -e- ro,

Duca:
La donna è mobile qual piuma al vento,
muta d'accento e di pensiero.

Sempre un amabile leggiadro viso, in
pianto o in riso, è menzognero.

Duke:
All women are capricious, like a plume in
the wind, changing their thoughts.

Their face is always amiable, but in tears
or in laughter, they are always deceptive.

È sempre misero chi a lei s'affida, chi le confida mal cauto il core!

Misfortune always awaits one who trusts them; one who confides in them must be cautious in his heart!

Pur mai non sentesi felice appieno chi su quel seno non liba amore!

But one can never achieve full happiness if he never tastes love!

Sparafucile places a flask of wine with two glasses on a table.
He then knocks on the ceiling twice with the hilt of his sword.
A smiling young gypsy woman descends the stairs.
The Duke rushes to embrace her, but she is coquettish and teases him.
Meanwhile, Sparafucile exits the Inn to speak with Rigoletto.

Sparafucile:
È là il vostr'uomo.
Viver dee o morire?

Sparafucile:
Your man is in there.
Shall he live or die?

Rigoletto:
Più tardi tornerò l'opra a compire.

Rigoletto:
I'll return later when the deed is accomplished.

Sparafucile goes off behind the house toward the river.
Gilda and Rigoletto remain outside the house.
They peer inside and overhear the Duke and Maddalena conversing.

Duca:
Un dì, si ben rammentomi, o bella, t'incontrai.
Mi piacque di te chiedere, e intesi che qui stai.
Or sappi, che d'allora sol te quest'alma adora.

Duke:
One day, if I remember well, beautiful lady, I met you.
I asked to know your name, and you intended to remain with me.
Your should know that from then on it is only you who I adore.

Gilda:
Iniquo!

Gilda:
Traitor!

Maddalena:
Ah, ah! E vent'altre appresso le scorda forse adesso?
Ha un'aria il signorino da vero libertino.

Maddalena:
Hah, hah! And later you seem to forget them all?
You have an air of a lord, a true libertine.

Duca:
Sì! Un mostro son.

Duke: *(trying to embrace her)*
Yes! I am a monster.

Gilda:
Ah padre mio!

Gilda: *(observing them)*
Oh father!

Maddalena:
Lasciatemi, stordito.

Maddalena:
Leave me, you inconsiderate man.

Duca:
Ah, che fracasso!

Duke:
Oh, what bickering!

Maddalena:
Stia saggio.

Maddalena:
This is nonsense.

Duca:
E tu sii docile,
non farmi tanto chiasso.
Ogni saggezza chiudesi nel gaudio e
nell'amore.

Duke:
And you are so gentle,
don't excite me so much.
Every wise indulges in the pleasures of
love.

The Duke takes Maddalena's hand.

La bella mano candida!.

Such a beautiful white hand!

Maddalena:
Scherzate voi, signore.

Maddalena:
You're playing games with me, sir.

Duca:
No, no.

Duke:
Not at all.

Maddalena:
Son brutta.

Maddalena:
I am ugly.

Duca:
Abbracciami.

Duke:
Embrace me.

Gilda:
Iniquo!

Gilda:
Betrayer!

Maddalena:
Ebro!

Maddalena:
You're drunk!

Duca:
D'amor ardente.

Duke: *(laughing)*
From ardent love.

Maddalena:
Signor l'indifferente, vi piace canzonar?

Maddalena:
Do you want me to sing?

Duca:
No, no, ti vo'sposar.

Duke:
No, no, I want to marry you.

Maddalena:
Ne voglio la parola.

Maddalena:
I don't want to hear that word.

Duca:
Amabile figliuola!

Duke: *(ironically)*
Such a gracious young woman!

Rigoletto:
E non ti basta ancor?

Rigoletto: *(to Gilda)*
Is that enough for you?

Gilda:
Iniquo traditor!

Gilda:
Wicked traitor!

Andante
DUKE

Bel- la figlia del-l'a - mo - re,   schiavo son de'vezzi   tuo - i,

Duca:
Bella figlia dell'amore, schiavo son
de'vezzi tuoi;
con un detto sol tu puoi le mie pene
consolar.
Vieni e senti del mio core il frequente
palpitar. Con un detto sol tu puoi le mie
pene consolar.

Duke:
Beautiful daughter of love, I am a slave to
you charms;
with one word you can console my
suffering.
Come and feel my heart pounding. With
one word, you can console my suffering.

Maddalena:
Ah! Ah! Rido ben di core, chè tai baie
costan poco, quanto valga il vostro gioco,
mel credete so apprezzar.
Sono avvezza, bel signore ad un simile
scherzar.

Maddalena:
Hah! Hah! My heart laughs, your jesting
is so casual, and your game so trivial. I
know well how to appreciate honey. I'm
accustomed to a handsome man and such
games.

Gilda:
Ah così parlar d'amore a me pur l'infame
ho udito!
Infelice cor tradito, per angoscia non
scoppiar.

Gilda:
The way he talks of love, I have truly
witnessed his betrayal!
Oh my unhappy betrayed heart. I don't
want to die of anguish.

Rigoletto:
Taci, il piangere non vale; ch'ei mentiva
or sei sicura.
Taci, e mia sarà la cura la vendetta
d'affrettar.
Sì, pronta fia sarà fatale, io saprollo
fulminar.

Rigoletto: *(to Gilda)*
Quiet, it's not worth tears; you can be
certain he is has lied to you.
Quiet, my cure will be a quick vengeance.
Yes, soon it will be fatal, and I will wield
it like a lightning bolt.

M'odì! Ritorna a casa oro prendi, un
destriero, una veste viril che t'apprestai,
e per Verona parti.
Sarovvi io pur doman.

Listen to me! Go home, take money, a
steed, a man's clothes to disguise
yourself, and go to Verona.
I'll meet you there tomorrow.

Gilda:
Or venite.

Gilda:
Come with me now.

Rigoletto:
Impossibil.

Rigoletto:
Impossible.

Gilda:
Tremo.

Gilda:
I'm afraid.

Rigoletto:
Va!

Rigoletto:
Go!

Gilda departs. The Duke and Maddalena remain in conversation inside the Inn.
Rigoletto goes behind the Inn and returns with Sparafucile,
and then counts out money for him.

Venti scudi hai tu detto?
Eccone dieci; e dopo l'opra il resto.
Ei qui rimane?

Did you say twenty scudos?
Here are ten; and after the deed the rest.
Will you be here?

Sparafucile:
Sì.

Sparafucile:
Yes.

Rigoletto:
Alla mezzanotte ritornerò.

Rigoletto:
I'll return at midnight.

Sparafucile:
Non cale. A gettarlo nel fiume basto io
solo.

Sparafucile:
It's not necessary. I can throw him in the
river myself.

Rigoletto:
No, no, il vo' far io stesso.

Rigoletto:
No, no, I want to do it myself.

Sparafucile:
Sia! Il suo nome?

Sparafucile:
All right! What's his name?

Rigoletto:
Vuoi saper anche il mio?
Egli è Delitto, Punizion son io.

Rigoletto:
Do you want to know mine too?
He is Crime, I am Punishment.

As Rigoletto departs, lightning flashes.

Sparafucile:
La tempesta è vicina!
Più scura fia la notte.

Sparafucile:
The storm is near!
The night is getting darker.

Duca:
Maddalena!

Duke: *(seizing Maddalena)*
Maddalena!

Maddalena:
Aspettate, mio fratello viene.

Maddalena: *(resisting him)*
Wait, my brother is coming.

Duca:
Che importa?

Duke:
Why should that matter?

Maddalena:
Tuona!

Maddalena:
There is thunder!

Sparafucile enters the Inn.

Sparafucile:
E pioverà fra poco.

Sparafucile:
It will be raining soon.

Duca:
Tanto meglio! Tu dormerai in scuderia,
all'inferno, ove vorrai.

Duke:
All the better! You sleep in the stable, or
with the devil, whatever you wish.

Sparafucile:
Oh grazie!

Sparafucile:
How gracious!

Maddalena:
(Ah, no, partite.)

Maddalena: *(aside to the Duke)*
(Oh, no, you must leave.)

Duca:
(Con tal tempo?)

Duke:
(You refuse me?)

Sparafucile:
Son venti scudi d'oro.

Sparafucile: *(aside to Maddalena)*
There are twenty scudos in gold.
(to the Duke)

Ben felice d'offrirvi la mia stanza, se a
voi piace tosto a vederla andiamo.

It will be my pleasure to offer you my
room, if you want to see it, let's go.

Sparafucile takes a light and goes toward the ladder leading to the second floor.

Duca:
Ebben!
Sono con te, presto, vediamo.

Duke:
Very well!
I'll go you, quickly, let's see.

The Duke whispers something to Maddalena and then follows Sparafucile.

Maddalena:
Povero giovin! Grazioso tanto!
Dio, qual notte è questa!

Maddalena:
That poor young man! So gracious!
God, what a dreadful night this is!

Duca:
Si dorme all'aria aperta?
Bene, Bene! Buona notte.

Duke: *(from upstairs)*
Sleeping in the open?
Good, good! Good evening.

Sparafucile:
Signor, vi guardi Iddio!

Sparafucile:
Sir, may God watch over you!

The Duke removes his hat and sword.

Duca:
Breve sonno dormiam, stanco son io.

Duke:
A short sleep, I'm quite tired.

La donna è mobile qual piuma al vento,
muta d'accento e di pensiero.

All women are capricious, like a plume in
the wind, changing their thoughts.

The Duke falls asleep. Meanwhile, Maddalena sits at a table with Sparafucile.
Sparafucile drinks from the bottle left by the Duke.
Both become preoccupied with serious thoughts, and then,
Maddalena breaks the silence.

Maddalena::
È amabile in vero cotal giovinotto!

Maddalena:
That young man is genuinely amiable!

Sparafucile:
Oh sì, venti scudi ne dà di prodotto.

Sparafucile:
Oh, yes, he's produced twenty scudos for
us.

Maddalena:
Sol venti? Son pochi!
Valeva di più.

Maddalena:
Only twenty? That's nothing!
He's worth more.

Sparafucile:
La spada, s'ei dorme, va portami giù.

Sparafucile:
My sword is idle, go get it for me.

Maddalena ascends the stairs and gazes at the Duke.

Maddalena:
Peccato è pur bello!

Maddalena:
It's a shame, he's so handsome!

Gilda appears outside the Inn. She is dressed in male clothes, with boots and spurs. She slowly approaches the Inn and observes Sparafucile.

Gilda:
Ah, più non ragiono!
Amor mi trascina!
Mio padre, perdono.
Qual notte d'orrore!
Gran Dio, che accadrà!

Gilda:
I can't bear it!
My lover has betrayed me!
Father, forgive me!
What a horrible night!
Oh, God, what a fate!

Maddalena returns to the ground floor and lays the Duke's sword on the table.

Maddalena:
Fratello?

Maddalena:
Brother?

Gilda:
Chi parla?

Gilda: *(spying on them)*
Who is that speaking?

Sparafucile:
Al diavol ten va

Sparafucile:
The devil awaits.

Maddalena:
Somiglia un Apollo quel giovine,
io l'amo, ei m'ama, riposi, nè più
l'uccidiamo.

Maddalena:
That young man looks like an Apollo.
I love him, and he loves me. Reconsider
and let's not kill him.

Gilda:
Oh cielo!

Gilda:
Oh Heavens!

Sparafucile:
Rattoppa quel sacco.

Sparafucile: *(throwing her a sack)*
Mend this sack.

Maddalena:
Perchè?

Maddalena:
Why?

Sparafucile:
Entr'esso il tuo Apollo, sgozzato da me,
gettar dovrò al fiume.

Sparafucile:
For your Apollo to be thrown in the river,
after I slaughter him.

Gilda:
L'inferno qui vedo!

Gilda:
I am witnessing hell!

Maddalena:
Eppure il danaro salvarti scommetto,
serbandolo in vita.

Sparafucile:
Difficile il credo.

Maddalena:
M'ascolta, anzi facil ti svelo un progetto.
De'scudi già dieci dal gobbo ne avesti;
venire cogl'altri più tardi il vedrai.
Uccidilo e, venti allora ne avrai.
Così tutto il prezzo goder si potrà.

Gilda:
Che sento! Mio padre!

Sparafucile:
Uccider quel gobbo!
Che diavol dicesti!
Un ladro son forse?
Son forse un bandito?
Qual altro cliente da me fu tradito?
Mi paga quest'uomo, fedele m'avrà.

Maddalena:
Ah, grazia per esso.

Sparafucile:
È duopo ch'ei muoia.

Maddalena:
Fuggire il fo adesso!

Gilda:
Oh buona figliuola!

Sparafucile:
Gli scudi perdiamo.

Maddalena:
È ver!

Sparafucile:
Lascia fare.

Maddalena:
If it was not for the money, I bet I could
persuade you to spare his life.

Sparafucile:
Don't even consider it.

Maddalena:
Listen to me. I have a better plan to you.
The hunchback already gave you ten
scudos, and he's coming later with the
rest. Kill him and then you'll have twenty.
It will be the full price and I'll be thrilled.

Gilda:
What do I hear! My father!

Sparafucile:
Kill the hunchback!
What devil speaks to me!
Am I a thief?
Am I a bandit?
Did I ever betray a client?
The man paid me and I must be honorable.

Maddalena:
Spare the young man.

Sparafucile:
I'll be killing him later.

Maddalena: *(rushing up the stairs)*
I'll let him escape from you!

Sparafucile:
Such a good woman!

Sparafucile:
We'll lose the money.

Maddalena:
That's true!

Sparafucile:
Let everything be.

Maddalena:
Salvarlo dobbiamo.

Maddalena:
We must save him.

Sparafucile:,
Se pria ch'abbia il mezzo la notte toccato
alcuno qui giunga, per esso morrà.

Sparafucile:
Then instead, whoever arrives here at
midnight will become the victim.

Maddalena:
È buoia la notte, il ciel troppo irato,
nessuno, a quest'ora da qui passerà.

Maddalena:
It's a dark night, and the Heaven's are
angry, no one will come here at this hour.

Gilda:
Oh qual tentazione!
Morir per l'ingrato!
Morire, mio padre! Oh cielo! Pietà!

Gilda:
What a temptation!
To die for that ingrate!
To die, father! Heaven! Mercy!

The violent thunder and lightning ceases. A clock strikes the half-hour.

Sparafucile:
Ancor c'è mezz'ora.

Sparafucile:
There's still a half-hour remaining.

Maddalena:
Attendi, fratello.

Maddalena: *(in tears)*
Wait, brother.

Gilda:
Che! Piange tal donna!
N'è a lui darò aita!
Ah, s'egli al mio amore divenne rubello,
io vo'per la sua gettar la mia vita.

Gilda:
What! A woman is in tears!
Can I let him perish?
Although he has betrayed our love,
I want to die for him.

Gilda knocks at the door.

Maddalena:
Si picchia?

Maddalena:
Who's knocking?

Sparafucile:
Fu il vento.

Sparafucile;
It was the wind.

Gilda knocks again.

Maddalena:
Si picchia, ti dico.

Maddalena:
I'm telling you someone is knocking.

Sparafucile:
È strano! Chi è?

Sparafucile:
That's strange! Who is it?

Gilda:
Pietà d'un mendico; asil per la notte a lui
concedete.

Maddalena:
Fia lunga tal notte!

Sparafucile:
Alquanto attendete.

Maddalena:
Su, spicciati, presto, fa l'opra compita;
anelo una vita con altra salvar.

Sparafucile:
Ebbene, son pronto, quell'uscio
dischiudi; più ch'altro gli scudi mi preme
salvar.

Gilda:
Ah! Presso alla morte, sì giovine, sono!
Oh ciel, per gl'empi ti chieggo perdono!
Perdona tu, o padre, questa infelice!
Sia l'uomo felice ch'or vado a salvar.

Gilda:
Mercy for a friar; please give him shelter
for the night.

Maddalena:
A stranger on such a night!

Sparafucile: *(searching the cupboard)*
I'll find something to give him.

Maddalena:
Get moving, quickly complete the job;
take a life so another can be saved.

Sparafucile:
Well, I'm ready, open the door; it is more
than money that's making me save your
prize.

Gilda:
I am about to die, my love!
Heaven, I ask your forgiveness!
Father, forgive this unhappy woman!
I save him to make him happy.

Amid thunder and lightning, Gilda knocks on the door again.
Sparafucile places himself behind the door, his dagger raised.

Sparafucile:
Apri.

Maddalena:
Entri.

Gilda:
Dio! Loro perdonate!

Sparafucile: *(to Maddalena)*
Open it.

Maddalena:
Come in.

Gilda:
God! Forgive me!

Gilda enters. Sparafucile closes the door behind her, and then stabs her.
The thunder ceases, but the rain and lightning continue.

In the darkness, there is silence. As the violent storm gradually abates,
Rigoletto, wrapped in his cloak, appears before the Inn.

Rigoletto:
Della vendetta alfin giunge l'istante!
Da trenta dì l'aspetto di vivo sangue a
lagrime piangendo, sotto la larva del
buffon.

Quest'uscio è chiuso!
Ah, non è tempo ancor!
S'attenda. Qual notte di mistero!
Una tempesta in cielo!
In terra un omicidio!
Oh come in vero qui grande mi sento!

Rigoletto:
The moment of vengeance finally arrives!
It has been thirty days of blood and
anguished tears beneath the jester's mask.

The door is closed!
There's not much time left!
I'll wait. What an ominous night!
A storm in the skies!
On earth a murder!
But truthfully, I feel wonderful!

The clock strikes midnight.

Mezza notte!   Midnight!

Rigoletto knocks on the door.

Sparafucile:
Chi è là?

Sparafucile:
Who is it?

Rigoletto:
Son io.

Rigoletto:
It is me.

Sparafucile brings the sack to Rigoletto.

Sparafucile:
Sostate.
È qua spento il vostr'uomo!

Sparafucile:
Wait.
Here is your dead man!

Rigoletto:
Oh gioia! Un lume!

Rigoletto:
What joy! A lamp!

Sparafucile:
Un lume? No, il danaro.
Lesti, all'onda il gettiam.

Sparafucile:
A lamp? No, the money.
Quickly, we'll throw him in the river.

Rigoletto:
No, basto io solo.

Rigoletto: *(gives him a purse)*
No, I will do that.

Sparafucile:
E come vi piace. Qui men atto è il sito più
avanti è più profondo il gorgo. Presto, che
alcun non vi sorprenda.
Buona notte.

Sparafucile:
At your pleasure. Here it is shallow, but
further down the river it is deeper.
Quickly, so no one surprises you.
Good evening.

Sparafucile reenters the Inn.

Rigoletto:

Egli è là! Morto! Oh sì! Vorrei vederlo!
Ma che importa! È ben desso!
Ecco i suoi sproni!
Ora mi guarda, o mondo!
Quest'è un buffone, ed un potente è
questo!
Ei sta sotto i miei piedi!
È desso! Oh gioia!
È giunta alfine la tua vendetta, o duolo!

Sia l'onda a lui sepolcro, un sacco il suo
lenzuolo! All'onda! All'onda!

Rigoletto:

He is dead! Yes! I want to see him!
But it's not important! It's surely him!
I feel his spurs!
Now world look at me!
This is a jester, and indeed a man of
power!
And he remains under my foot!
It is true! What joy!
My greed has vanished, my vengeance
finally has arrived!
The waves will be his grave, the sack his
shroud! To the waves! To the waves!

As Rigoletto drags the sack toward the river,
he is shocked when he hears the voice of the Duke in the distance.

Duca:

La donna è mobile qual piuma al vento,
muta d'accento e di pensiero.
Sempre un amabile leggiadro viso, in
pianto o in riso, è menzognero.

La donna è mobile qual piuma al vento,
muta d'accento e di pensiero.

Duke:

All women are capricious, like a plume in
the wind, changing their thoughts.
Their face is always amiable, but
deceptive in their tears or laughter.

All women are capricious, like a plume in
the wind, changing tone and thought.

Rigoletto:

Qual voce! Illusion notturna è questa!
No, no! Egli è desso!
Maledizione!

Rigoletto:

That voice! It's an illusion of the night!
No, no! He's in here!
Curses!

Rigoletto rushes toward the Inn and knocks on the door.

Olà, dimon bandito!
Chi è mai, chi è qui in sua vece?

Io tremo, è umano corpo!

Hello, demonic bandit!
Who is it, who is in the sack?

I'm trembling, it's a human body!

Rigoletto cuts open the sack. There is a flash of lightning revealing Gilda.

Mia figlia! Dio! Mia figlia!
Ah, no! È impossibil!
Per Verona è in via!
Fu vision! È dessa!

Oh mia Gilda! Fanciulla a me rispondi!
L'assassino mi svela.

My daughter! My daughter!
No! It's impossible!
She's en route to Verona!
It was a vision! But it is her!

My Gilda! Girl answer me!
Tell me who the assassin was.

Rigoletto knocks desperately at the door of the Inn.

Olà? Nessuno! Nessun! | Hello? No one! No one!
Mia figlia? Mia Gilda? | My daughter? My daughter?
Oh mia figlia? | Oh, my daughter?

Gilda:
Chi mi chiama?

Gilda:
Who calls me?

Rigoletto:
Ella parla! Si move!
È viva! Oh Dio!
Ah, mio ben solo in terra mi guarda, mi conosci.

Rigoletto:
She speaks! She moves!
She is alive! Oh God!
Look at me, my only treasure, recognize me.

Gilda:
Ah, padre mio!

Gilda:
Oh, my father!

Rigoletto:
Qual mistero! Che fu!
Sei tu ferita? Dimmi.

Rigoletto:
What a mystery! By whom!
Are you wounded? Tell me.

Gilda:
L'acciar qui, qui mi piagò.

Gilda: *(indicating her heart)*
The wound, here is where it struck.

Rigoletto:
Chi t'ha colpita?

Rigoletto:
Who struck you?

Andante
GILDA

V'ho ingannato colpevole fu - i   *l'amai troppo ora muoio per lu - i!*

Gilda:
V'ho l'ingannato, colpevole fui, l'amai troppo, ora muoio per lui!

Gilda:
I have deceived you. I was guilty. I loved him too much. Now I die for him!

Rigoletto:
(Dio tremendo! Ella stessa fu côlta dallo stral di mia giusta vendetta!)

Rigoletto:
(Frightful God! She herself was struck by the darts of my righteous vengeance!)

Angiol caro, mi guarda, m'ascolta, parla, parlami, figlia diletta!

Dear angel, look at me, listen to me, speak, speak to me, precious daughter!

Gilda:
Ah, ch'io taccia! A me, a lui perdonate!
Benedite, alla figlia, o mio padre.

Gilda:
I accuse myself! Forgive him for me!
Oh father, bless your daughter.

Andante
GILDA

Lassù in cielo, vi - ci-no al -la madre,   in   e   -   terno per voi preghiero,

Lassù in cielo, vicina alla madre, in eterno
per voi pregherò.

Up there, in Heaven, near my mother,
I will forever pray for you.

Rigoletto:
Non morir mio tesoro, pietade mia
colomba lasciarmi non dêi.

Rigoletto:
Don't die my treasure, have pity my dove,
don't leave me.

Se t'involi qui sol rimarrei non morire,
o qui teco morrò!

If you leave me here alone I will mourn,
don't die, or I will also die!

Gilda:
Non più. A lui perdonate mio padre, ad...
dio!

Gilda:
I can't anymore. Forgive him father,
fare..well!

Gilda dies.

Rigoletto:
Gilda! Mia Gilda! È morta!
Ah! La maledizione!!

Rigoletto:
Gilda! My Gilda! She is dead!
Ah! The curse!

Rigoletto tears at his hair, and then faints as he falls on Gilda's corpse.

Made in United States
Troutdale, OR
01/02/2025

27529375R00037